Forew

This book gives you the opportunity to take guidance from successful people via their life story and/or their mind set.

At some point in our lives, we all need a boost to take us to the next level. This book is designed to do just that.

Whenever you feel as though your life is stagnating and going nowhere, then the chapters within will give you the inspiration and drive to move forward.

Each chapter highlights a famous and successful person who can motivate you and your life. Included are ten of their favourite quotes for you to read and be inspired by.

Please enjoy the book and take the first step to creating the life you dream of.

Paul Abraham

Chapter listing

1. Positivity – Nelson Mandela

2. Inspiration – Greta Thunberg

3. Business – Colonel Sanders

4. Challenges – Amy Johnson

5. Champions – Sir Alex Ferguson

6. Success – Oprah Winfrey

7. Winning – Vince Lombardi

8. Goals – Usain Bolt

9. Determination – Soichiro Honda

10. Motivation – Anthony Robbins

Positivity

Definition

According to the Oxford
English Dictionary definition, **positivity** is: "The practice of
being or tendency to be positive or optimistic in attitude."
That's right. **Positivity** is a practice, not something you're
born with.

Nelson Mandela

Throughout his 27 years in jail Nelson Mandela always remained **positive** that one day South Africa would rid itself of the cancer that was aphartied.

Rolihlahla Mandela was born into the Madiba clan in the village of Myezo, in the Eastern Cape, on 18 July 1918..

Hearing the elders' stories of his ancestors' valour during the wars of resistance, he dreamed also of making his own contribution to the freedom struggle of his people.

In 1961, Mandela orchestrated a three-day national workers' strike. He was arrested for leading the strike the following year and was sentenced to five years in prison. In 1963, Mandela was brought to trial again. This time, he and 10 other ANC leaders were sentenced to life imprisonment for political offenses, including sabotage.

Mandela spent 27 years in prison, from November 1962 until February 1990. He was incarcerated on Robben Island for 18 of his 27 years in prison. During this time, he contracted tuberculosis and, as a Black political prisoner, received the lowest level of treatment from prison workers. However, while incarcerated, Mandela was able to earn a Bachelor of Law degree through a University of London correspondence program.

A 1981 memoir by South African intelligence agent Gordon Winter described a plot by the South African government to arrange for Mandela's escape so as to shoot him during the recapture; the plot was foiled by British intelligence.

Mandela continued to be such a potent and positive symbol of Black resistance that a coordinated international campaign for his release was launched, and this international groundswell of support exemplified the power and esteem that Mandela had in the global political community.

In 1982, Mandela and other ANC leaders were moved to Pollsmoor Prison, allegedly to enable contact between them and the South African government. In 1985, President P.W. Botha offered Mandela's release in exchange for renouncing armed struggle; the prisoner flatly rejected the offer. With increasing local and international pressure for his release, the government participated in several talks with Mandela over the ensuing years, but no deal was made.

On 12 August 1988 he was taken to hospital where he was diagnosed with tuberculosis. After more than three months in two hospitals he was transferred on 7 December 1988 to a house at Victor Verster Prison near Paarl where he spent his last 14 months of imprisonment. He was released from its gates on Sunday 11 February 1990, nine days after the unbanning of the ANC and the PAC and nearly four months after the release of his remaining Rivonia comrades. Throughout his imprisonment he had rejected at least three conditional offers of release.

Upon his release from prison, Mandela immediately urged foreign powers not to reduce their pressure on the South African government for constitutional reform. While he stated that he was committed to working toward peace, he declared that the ANC's armed struggle would continue until the Black majority received the right to vote.

In 1991, Mandela was elected president of the African National Congress, with lifelong friend and colleague Oliver Tambo serving as national chairperson. In 1993, Mandela and President de Klerk were jointly awarded the Nobel Peace Prize for their work toward dismantling apartheid in South Africa.

On 10 May 1994 he was inaugurated as South Africa's first democratically elected President. On his 80th birthday in 1998 he married Graça Machel, his third wife.

True to his promise, Mandela stepped down in 1999 after one term as President. He continued to work with the Nelson Mandela Children's Fund he set up in 1995 and established the Nelson Mandela Foundation and The Mandela Rhodes Foundation.

In April 2007 his grandson, Mandla Mandela, was installed as head of the Mvezo Traditional Council at a ceremony at the Mvezo Great Place.

Nelson Mandela never wavered in his devotion to democracy, equality and learning. Despite terrible provocation, he never answered racism with racism. His life is an inspiration to all who are oppressed and deprived; and to all who are opposed to oppression and deprivation.

He died at his home in Johannesburg on 5 December 2013.

Top ten Nelson Mandela quotes

1. "Everyone can rise above their circumstances and achieve success if they are dedicated to and passionate about what they do."

2. "It always seems impossible, until it is done."

3. "Lead from the back – and let others believe they are in front."

4. "What counts in life is not the mere fact that we have lived. It is what difference we have made to the lives of others that will determine the significance of the life we lead."

5. "I am fundamentally an optimist. Part of being optimistic is keeping one's head pointed toward the sun, one's feet moving forward. There were many dark moments when my faith in humanity was sorely tested, but I would not and could not give myself up to despair. That way lays defeat and death."

6. "Education is the most powerful weapon which you can use to change the world."

7. "Do not judge me by my successes, judge me by how many times I fell down and got back up again."

8. "We must use time wisely and forever realize that the time is always ripe to do right."

9. "I like friends who have independent minds because they tend to make you see problems from all angles."

10. "No one is born hating another person because of the colour of his skin, or his background, or his religion. People must learn to hate, and if they can learn to hate, they can be taught to love, for love comes more naturally to the human heart than its opposite."

Inspiration

Definition

Inspiration is a feeling of enthusiasm you get from someone or something, that gives you new and creative ideas. ... If you describe someone or something good as an **inspiration**, you mean that they make you or other people want to do or achieve something.

Greta Thunberg

The OOOM 100 jury voted Greta Thunberg to the top of the ranking of "The World's Most **Inspiring** People 2019," honouring her unrelenting fight for the planet. Thunberg proves to all of us that every person has the power to change the world.

Greta Thunberg was born on 3 January 2003 in Stockholm, Sweden,

Thunberg says she first heard about climate change in 2011, when she was eight years old, and could not understand why so little was being done about it. The situation made her depressed. She stopped talking and eating, and lost ten kilograms (22 lb) in two months. Greta struggled with depression for three or four years before she began her school strike. Eventually, she was diagnosed with Asperger syndrome, OCD and selective Mutism. In one of her first speeches demanding climate action, Thunberg described the selective mutism aspect of her condition as meaning she "only speaks when necessary".

In August 2018, Thunberg began the school climate strikes and public speeches for which she has become an internationally recognised climate activist. In May 2018, Thunberg won a climate change essay competition held by Swedish newspaper Svenska Dagbladet. In part, she wrote "I want to feel safe. How can I feel safe when I know we are in the greatest crisis in human history?" After the paper published her article, it was suggested that school children could strike for climate change. Thunberg tried to persuade other young people to get involved but "no one was really interested", so eventually she decided to go ahead with the strike by herself. On 20 August 2018, Thunberg, who had just started ninth grade, decided not to attend school until the 2018 Swedish general election on 9 September. Thunberg said her teachers were divided in their views about her missing class to make her point. She says: "As people they think what I am doing is good, but as teachers they say I should stop."

Thunberg posted a photo of her first strike day on Instagram and Twitter, with other social media accounts quickly taking up her cause. High-profile youth activists amplified her Instagram post, and on the second day she was joined by other activists. A representative of the Finnish bank Nordea quoted one of Thunberg's tweets to more than 200,000 followers. Thunberg's social media profile attracted local reporters whose stories earned international coverage in little more than a week.

After October 2018, Thunberg's activism evolved from solitary protesting to taking part in demonstrations throughout Europe; making several high-profile public speeches, and mobilising her growing number of followers on social media platforms. After the December 2018 general elections, Thunberg continued to strike only on Fridays. She inspired school students across the globe to take part in student strikes. That month, more than 20,000 students had held strikes in at least 270 cities. Her speech during the plenary session of the 2018 United Nations Climate Change Conference (COP24) went viral. She commented that the world leaders present were "not mature enough to tell it like it is". In the first half of 2019 she joined various student protests around Europe, and was invited to speak at various forums and parliaments. At the January 2019 World Economic Forum, Thunberg gave a speech in which she declared: "Our house is on fire".

She addressed the British, European and French parliaments, where in the latter case several right-wing politicians boycotted her. In a short meeting with Thunberg, Pope Francis thanked her and encouraged her to continue. By March 2019, Thunberg was still staging her regular protests outside the Swedish parliament every Friday, where other students occasionally joined her. According to her father, her activism has not interfered with her schoolwork, but she has had less spare time. She finished lower secondary school with good grades. In July 2019, *Time* magazine reported Thunberg was taking a "sabbatical year" from school, intending to travel in the Americas while meeting people from the climate movement.

In August 2019, Thunberg sailed across the Atlantic Ocean from Plymouth, England, to New York, USA, in the 60-foot (18 m) racing yacht *Malizia II*, equipped with solar panels and underwater turbines. The trip was announced as a carbon-neutral transatlantic crossing serving as a demonstration of Thunberg's declared beliefs of the importance of reducing emissions. The voyage lasted fifteen days, from 14 to 28 August 2019. Thunberg was invited to give testimony in the US House Select Committee on the Climate Crisis on September 18.

Instead of giving testimony, she gave an eight sentence statement and submitted the IPCC Special Report on Global Warming of 1.5 C as evidence.

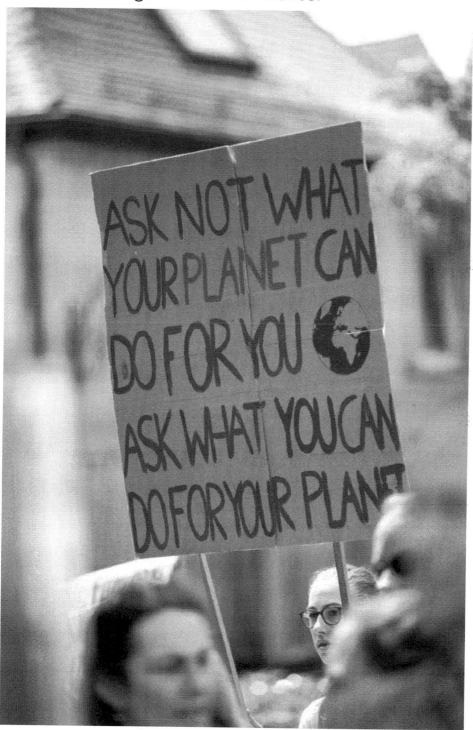

Top ten Greta Thunberg quotes

1. "We will never forgive you"

2. "The eyes of all future generations are upon you. And if you choose to fail us, I say – "My message is that we'll be watching you. This is all wrong. I shouldn't be up here. I should be back in school on the other side of the ocean. Yet you all come to us young people for hope. How dare you. You have stolen my dreams and my childhood with your empty words. Yet I am one of the lucky ones. People are suffering."

3. "We showed that we are united and that we, young people, are unstoppable"

4. "We are striking because we have done our homework, and they have not"

5. "Since our leaders are behaving like children, we will have to take the responsibility they should have taken long ago"

6. "I want you to act as if the house is on fire, because it is"

7. "The moment we decide to fulfil something, we can do anything"

8. "When haters go after your looks and differences, it means they have nowhere left to go. And then you know you're winning!"

9. "You must unite behind the science. You must take action. You must do the impossible. Because giving up can never ever be an option"

10. "Change is coming, whether you like it or not"

Business

Definition

Like everything else with your **business**, it's up to you to define what **success** is. ... **Success** is running a profitable firm that conducts **business** with honesty and integrity, makes meaningful contributions to the communities it serves, and nurtures high-quality, balanced lives for its employees,

Colonel Sanders

He was a broke, alone, 65 year-old looking at his first Social Security cheque for $105, his name? Colonel Sanders. He started thinking of ways to boost his income, but all he had was a chicken recipe that everyone who'd tasted it, seemed to like. If he sold his recipe to restaurants, that would barely pay his rent, could he sell the recipe and show restaurants how to cook the chicken properly, while taking a percentage of profits if **business** was increased due to his recipe? He went knocking on doors, telling each restaurant owner his idea, many just laughed in his face and told him to go and take his stupid idea with him.

Instead of giving up, after each refusal he focused on how to approach the next restaurant with a different sales pitch. He spent two years driving across American in his old beaten up car and rumpled white suit while using the back seat as a bed. Colonel Sanders idea was turned down 1,009 times, yes, 1,009 time people said "no" before he finally had a chance to fulfil his **business** ambition, and as they say "the rest is history"!

Top ten Colonel Sanders quotes

1. "One has to remember that every failure can be a stepping-stone to something better"
2. "I just say the moral out of my life is don't quit at age 65, maybe your boat hasn't come in yet. Mine hadn't." (On not starting KFC until he was 65 and selling it for $2 million in 1964)
3. "The easy way rests hazardously upon shifting sands, whereas the hard way builds solidly a foundation."
4. "Have ambition to work, willingness to work and integrity in what you do."
5. "You've got to like your work. You've got to like what you are doing, you've got to be doing something worthwhile so you can like it – because if it's worthwhile, that makes a difference, don't you see?"
6. "Where either you're on your own job or you're dreaming about different things and you can always take something in your life and make it better."
7. "I had a moral obligation to give people something good. Something worthwhile. I loved it."
8. "I made a resolve then that I was going to amount to something if I could. And no hours, nor amount of labour, nor amount of money would deter me from giving the best that there was in me. And I have done that ever since, and I win by it. I know."
9. "There's no reason to be the richest man in the cemetery. You can't do any business from there."

10. "] Don't worry about this rain as some farmer is happy to have this rain."

Challenges

Definition

The situation of being faced with) something that needs
great mental or physical effort in order to be done
successfully and therefore tests a person's ability: Finding
a solution to this problem is one of the
greatest **challenges** faced by the human race today.

Amy Johnson

The **challenge** of flying solo from England to Australia in 1930, was an achievement for any experienced male aviators, so Amy Johnson becoming the first female to complete the journey in those male dominated times is even more remarkable.

Born in Hull in 1903, Amy left the University of Sheffield with a Bachelor of Arts degree in economics and became a solicitor's secretary in London. She was introduced to flying as an exciting hobby and gained her pilots "A" licence 5 days after her 26th birthday at the London Aeroplane club.

With £600 from her father and Lord Wakefield she purchased "*G-AAAH*", a second-hand de Havilland DH60 Gipsy Moth which she named "Jason". Amy was soon looking for more and more **challenges** and received worldwide recognition when, in 1930 she became the first female pilot, to fly solo from England to Australia. Flying "Jason", she left Croydon on the 5th May, and landed in Darwin, Northern Territory, on May 24th after flying 11,000 miles. She received the Harmon Trophy as well as a CBE in recognition of this achievement, and was honoured with the No. 1 Civil Pilots licence under Australia's 1921 Air Navigation Regulations.

In 1932 Amy married Scottish pilot Jim Mollison, who had, during a flight together, proposed to her only eight hours after they had met. In July of the same year, Amy set a solo record for the flight from London to Cape Town, South Africa in a Puss Moth, "G-ACAB" named "Desert Cloud", breaking her new husband's record.

The Second World War saw Amy (now divorced) join the Air Transport Auxiliary, with her duties consisted of ferrying aircraft from factory airstrips to RAF bases. It was on one of these routine flights on 5th January 1941, that Amy crashed in to the Thames estuary and was drowned; her body was never recovered. Mystery still surrounds her death with the reason for her flight remaining a government secret.

Top ten Amy Johnson quotes

1. "Had I been a man I might have explored the Poles or climbed Mount Everest, but as it was my spirit found outlet in the air."

2. "I think it is a pity to lose the romantic side of flying and simply to accept it as a common means of transport, although that end is what we have all ostensibly been striving to attain."

3. "This book is dedicated to all those who fell by the airside, for nothing is wasted, and every apparent failure is but a challenge to others."

4. "The more positive you feel about yourself, the less anxious you feel - and will tend to stutter less."

5. "Tired of trying to sort them out, you relax for a second, then your head drops and you sit up with a jerk, Where are you? What are you doing here?" Oh yes, of course, you are somewhere in the middle of the North Atlantic, with hungry waves below you like vultures impatiently waiting for the end."

6. "We are pretty solid. It all depends on how this team comes together"

7. "One would think it'd be uncomfortable for the guys, but the more they make us laugh the better."

8. "I believe I can do anything. If I decide I want to be a doctor tomorrow, I'm going to be a doctor."

9. "The point is to be ok with your stuttering – meet adults who stutter who are doctors, lawyers or engineers"

10. "Setting off unknown to face the unknown, against parental opposition, with no money, friends, or influence, ran it a close second. Clichés like "blazing trails," flying over "shark-infected seas," "battling with monsoons," and "forced landings amongst savage tribes" became familiar diet for breakfast."

Champions

Definition

A person or team who has surpassed all rivals in a
sporting contest or other competition.

Sir Alex Ferguson,

A former Scottish football manager and player Alex managed Manchester United from 1986 to 2013. He is regarded by many players, managers and analysts to be one of the greatest and most successful managers of all time.

Ferguson played as a forward for several Scottish clubs, including Dunfermline Athletic and Rangers. While playing for Dunfermline, he was the top goalscorer in the Scottish league in the 1965–66 season. Towards the end of his playing career he also worked as a coach, then started his managerial career with East Stirlingshire and St Mirren. Ferguson then enjoyed a highly successful period as manager of Aberdeen, winning three Scottish league **championships**, four Scottish Cups and the UEFA Cup Winners' Cup in 1983. He briefly managed Scotland following the death of Jock Stein, taking the team to the 1986 World Cup.

Ferguson was appointed manager of Manchester United in November 1986. During his 26 years with Manchester United he won 38 trophies, including 13 Premier League titles, five FA Cups and two UEFA **Champions** League titles. He was knighted in the 1999 Queen's Birthday Honours list, for his services to the game. Ferguson is the longest serving manager of Manchester United, having overtaken Sir Matt Busby's record on 19 December 2010. He retired from management at the end of the 2012–13 season, having won the Premier League in his final season.

Top ten "Fergie" quotes

1. "The work of a team should always embrace a great player but the great player must always work."

2. "I'm going to tell you the story about the geese which fly 5,000 miles from Canada to France. They fly in V-formation but the second ones don't fly. They're the subs for the first ones. And then the second ones take over - so it's teamwork."

3. "I used to have a saying that when a player is at his peak, he feels as though he can climb Everest in his slippers."

4. "There is no room for criticism on the training field. For a player – and for any human being – there is nothing better than hearing 'well done'. Those are the two best words ever invented in sports. You don't need to use superlatives."

5. "There's a reason that God gave us two ears, two eyes, and one mouth. It's so you can listen and watch twice as much as you talk. Best of all, listening costs you nothing."

6. "The experience of defeat, or more particularly the manner in which a leader reacts to it, is an essential part of what makes a winner."

7. "For me, drive means a combination of a willingness to work hard, emotional fortitude, enormous powers of concentration and a refusal to admit defeat."

8. "Part of the pursuit of excellence involves eliminating as many surprises as possible because life is full of the unexpected."

9. "There's a lot of satisfaction that comes from knowing you're doing your best and there's even more that comes when it begins to pay off"

10. "You cannot lead by following"

Success

Definition

Success (the opposite of failure) is the status of having achieved and accomplished an aim or objective. Being **successful** means the achievement of desired visions and planned goals.

Ophra Winfey

Born in rural poverty on January 29, 1954 and raised by a mother dependent on government welfare payments in a poor urban neighbourhood, At high school she **successfully** won an oratory contest, which secured her a full scholarship to Tennessee State University, a historically black institution, where she studied communication. Her first job as a teenager was working at a local grocery store. At the age of 17, Winfrey won the Miss Black Tennessee beauty pageant. She also attracted the attention of the local black radio station, WVOL, which hired her to do the news part-time. She worked there during her senior year of high school and in her first two years of college.

Winfrey's career in media would not have surprised her grandmother, who once said that ever since Winfrey could talk, she was on stage. As a child, she played games interviewing her corncob doll and the crows on the fence of her family's property. Winfrey later acknowledged her grandmother's influence, saying it was Hattie Mae who had encouraged her to speak in public and "gave me a positive sense of myself"

Working in local media, she was both the youngest news anchor and the first black female news anchor at Nashville's WLAC-TV. In 1976, she moved to Baltimore's WJZ-TV to co-anchor the six o'clock news. In 1977, she was removed as co-anchor and worked in lower profile positions at the station. She was then recruited to join Richard Sher as co-host of WJZ's local talk show "People Are Talking", which premiered on August 14, 1978.

In 1983, Winfrey relocated to Chicago to host WLS-TV's low-rated half-hour morning talk show, *AM Chicago*. The first episode aired on January 2, 1984. Within months after Winfrey took over, the show went from last place in the ratings to overtaking Donahue as the highest-rated talk show in Chicago. The movie critic Roger Ebert persuaded her to sign a syndication deal with King World . Ebert predicted that she would generate 40 times as much revenue as his television show, "At the Movies" It was then renamed The Oprah Winfrey Show and expanded to a full hour. The first episode was broadcast nationwide on September 8, 1986. Winfrey's syndicated show brought in double Donahue's national audience, displacing Donahue as the number-one daytime talk show in America.

Winfrey's continued **success** enabled her to become a millionaire at the age of 32 when her talk show received national syndication. Winfrey negotiated ownership rights to the television program and started her own production company. At the age of 41, Winfrey had a net worth of $340 million and replaced Bill Cosby as the only African American on the Forbes 400. By 2000, with a net worth of $800 million, Winfrey is believed to have been the richest African American of the 20th century. There has been a course taught at the University of Illinois focusing on Winfrey's business acumen, namely: "History 298: Oprah Winfrey, the Tycoon". Winfrey was the highest paid television entertainer in the United States in 2006, earning an estimated $260 million during the year, five times the sum earned by second-place music executive Simon Cowell By 2008, her yearly income had increased to $275 million.

Forbes' list of The Worlds Billionaires has listed Winfrey as the world's only black billionaire from 2004 to 2006 and as the first black woman billionaire in the world that was achieved in 2003.

On January 15, 2008, Winfrey and Discovery Communications announced plans to change Discovery Health Channel into a new channel called OWN: Oprah Winfrey Network. It was scheduled to launch in 2009 but was delayed, and actually launched on January 1, 2011.

In January 2017, CBS announced that Winfrey would join "60 Minutes" as a special contributor on the Sunday evening news magazine program starting in September 2017. The National Museum of African American History and Culture in 2018 opened a special exhibit on Winfrey's cultural influence through television. Winfrey left *60 Minutes* by the end of 2018

In June 2018, Apple announced a multi-year content partnership with Winfrey, in which it was agreed that Winfrey would create new original programs exclusively for Apple's streaming service, Apple TV+ The first show under the deal, Oprah's Book Club premiered on November 1, 2019. *Oprah's Book Club* is based on the segment of the same name from the Oprah Winfrey Show.

Top ten Oprah Winfrey quotes

1. "Turn your wounds into wisdom."
2. "Be thankful for what you have; you'll end up having more. If you concentrate on what you don't have, you will never, ever have enough"
3. "True forgiveness is when you can say, "Thank you for that experience."
4. "Real integrity is doing the right thing, knowing that nobody's going to know whether you did it or not."
5. "Breathe. Let go. And remind yourself that this very moment is the only one you know you have for sure."
6. "The more you praise and celebrate your life, the more there is in life to celebrate."
7. "Surround yourself only with people who are going to take you higher."
8. "You don't become what you want, you become what you believe."
9. "Challenges are gifts that force us to search for a new centre of gravity. Don't fight them. Just find a new way to stand."
10. "When you undervalue what you do, the world will undervalue who you are."

Winning

Definition

The success and achievement of goals and targets help to reinforce and confirm their self-belief. **Winners** are also self-aware: they know their limits and accept their imperfections, choosing to build on their personal Strengths and self-improve in order to achieve their successes.

Vince Lombardi

Vince was an American football player, coach, and executive in the National Football League (NFL). He is best known as the head coach of the Green Bay Packers during the 1960s, where he led the team to three straight and five total NFL Championships in seven years, in addition to **winning** the first two Super Bowls following the 1966 and 1967 NFL seasons. Lombardi is considered by many to be one of the best and most successful coaches in professional football history. The NFL's Super Bowl trophy is named in his honour. He was enshrined in the Pro Football Hall of Fame in 1971, the year after his death.

Lombardi began coaching as an assistant and later as a head coach at St. Cecilia High School in Englewood, New Jersey. He was an assistant coach at Fordham, at the United States Military Academy, and with the New York Giants before becoming a head coach for the Green Bay Packers from 1959 to 1967 and the Washington Redskins in 1969. He never had a losing season as a head coach in the NFL, compiling a regular season **winning** percentage of 72.8 (96–34–6), and 90% (9–1) in the postseason for an overall record of 105 wins, 35 losses, and 6 ties in the NFL.

His comments and motivational ideas are still used by leading sports and business coaches around the world, fifty years after his death.

Top ten Vince Lombardi quotes.

1. "Perfection is not something to aim for because it is impossible to be perfect. However, if we are constantly chasing perfection we can end up reaching excellence. Excellence is something all humans should strive for in every endeavour we choose."

2. "It's not whether you get knocked down; it's whether you get up."

3. "Individual commitment to a group effort – that is what makes a team work, a company work, a society work, a civilization work."

4. "The only place success comes before work is in the dictionary."

5. "Winners never quit, and quitters never win."

6. "Practice doesn't make perfect. Perfect practice makes perfect."

7. "The achievements of an organization are the results of the combined effort of each individual."

8. "The greatest accomplishment is not in never failing, but in rising against after you fail."

9. "The price of success is hard work, dedication to the job, and determination"

10. "The spirit, the will to win, and the will to excel are the things that endure"

Goals

Definition

The **definition of goal setting** is the process of identifying something that you want to accomplish and establishing measurable **goals** and timeframes. When you decide on a financial change to save more money and then **set** a certain amount to save each month, this is an example of **goal setting**.

Usain Bolt

At the launch of his autobiography 'Faster Than Lightning' in London, Usain told the crowd present that "If you want to be the best, or you want to strive for more, you've got to set goals in life."

Bolt was born on August 21,1986, in Jamaica. Both a standout cricket player and a sprinter early on, Bolt's natural speed was noticed by coaches at school, and he began to focus solely on sprinting under the tutelage of Pablo McNeil, a former Olympic sprint athlete. (Glen Mills would later serve as Bolt's coach and mentor.) As early as age 14, Bolt was wowing fans with his lightning speed, and he won his first high school championship medal in 2001, taking the silver in the 200-meter race.

At the age of 15, Bolt took his first shot at success on the world stage at the 2002 World Junior Championships in Kingston, Jamaica, where he won the 200-meter dash, making him the youngest world-junior gold medalist ever. Bolt's feats impressed the sports world, and he received the International Association of Athletics Foundation's Rising Star Award that year, boosting the recognition of a young man soon to be known as "Lightning Bolt."

Bolt reached the world Top 5 rankings in 2005 and 2006. Unfortunately, injuries continued to plague the 6'5" sprinter, preventing him from completing a full professional season. In 2007, Bolt broke the national 200-meter record held for over 30 years by Donald Quarrie, and earned two silver medals at the World Championships in Osaka, Japan. These medals boosted Bolt's desire to run, and he took a more serious stance toward his career.

At the 2008 Beijing Summer Olympics, Bolt ran the 100-meter and 200-meter events. In the 100-meter final leading up to the Games, he broke the world record, winning in 9.69 seconds. Not only was the record set without a favourable wind, but he also visibly slowed down to celebrate before he finished (and his shoelace was untied), an act that aroused much controversy later on. He went on to win three gold medals and break three world records in Beijing.

At the 2012 Summer Olympic Games, held in London, Bolt won his fourth Olympic gold medal in the men's 100-meter race, beating rival Yohan Blake, who won silver in the event. Bolt ran the race in 9.63 seconds, a new Olympic record. The win marked Bolt's second consecutive gold medal in the 100. He went on to compete in the men's 200, claiming his second consecutive gold medal in that race as well. He became the first man to win both the 100 and 200 in consecutive Olympic Games, as well as the first man to ever win back-to-back gold medals in double sprints. Bolt's accomplishments made him the first man in history to set three world records in a single Olympic Games competition.

Bolt returned to Olympic glory at the 2016 Summer Olympic Games when he won gold in the 100-meter race, making him the first athlete to win three successive titles in the event. He finished the race in 9.81 seconds with American runner and rival Justin Gatlin, who took silver, 0.08 seconds behind him.

"This is why I came here, to the Olympics, to prove to the world that I'm the best — again," he told reporters at a news conference. "It always feels good to go out on top, you know what I mean?"

He continued his Olympic winning streak, taking gold in the 200 meters in 19.78 seconds. "What else can I do to prove I am the greatest?" Bolt said in an interview with BBC Sport. "I'm trying to be one of the greatest, to be among Muhammad Ali and Pele, I have made the sport exciting, I have made people want to see the sport. I have put the sport on a different level."

The "fastest man alive" remained undefeated in what he said would be the last race of his Olympic career, the 4x100-meter relay, which he ran with teammates Blake, Asafa Powell and Nickel Ashmeade. Anchoring the race, Bolt led the Jamaican team to gold, crossing the finish line in 37.27 seconds. It was the third consecutive gold medal win for Bolt in Rio.

Bolt is an 11-time world champion. He holds the world records in races for 100 meters, at 9.58 seconds, and 200 meters, at 19.19 seconds, both of which he set at the

2009 Berlin World Athletics Championships. Over the course of his career, Bolt has received numerous awards, including the IAAF World Athlete of the Year (twice), Track & Field Athlete of the Year and Laureus Sportsman of the Year.

Participating in the 2008, 2012 and 2016 summer Olympic Games, Bolt completed a "triple-triple," with a total of nine gold medals earned in the 100-meter, 200-meter and 4x100-meter relay races. In doing so, Bolt joined just two other triple-triple runners: Paavo Nurmi of Finland (in 1920, 1924 and 1928) and Carl Lewis of the United States (in 1984, 1988, 1992 and 1996). However in January 2017, the International Olympic Committee stripped Bolt of one of these medals, for the 2008 4x100-meter relay, because his teammate Nesta Carter was found guilty of a doping violation.

Bolt took back the 100-meter world title on August 11, 2013, after having lost the title in 2011. Although Bolt didn't strike his signature "lightning bolt" pose after the race, his winning image still caused a stir, with lightning striking just as he crossed the finish line.

In 2015, Bolt faced some challenges: He came in second at the Nassau IAAF World Relays in May, but secured an individual win in the 200-meter event at the Ostrava Golden Spike event that same month. He also dominated the 200-meter race at the New York Addias Grand Prix that June. Trouble with his pelvic muscles forced him to withdraw from two races, though Bolt made a comeback that July with a 100-meter win at London's Anniversary Games.

In 2017, Bolt faced challenges on the track at the World Athletics Championships. He finished third in the men's 100 meters, taking home the bronze medal behind Christian Coleman, who won silver, and Gatlin, who took home the gold. It was the first time that Bolt had been beaten at the World Athletics Championships since 2007. His struggles didn't end there: In the 4x100-meter relay, which many believed would be Bolt's final race, he collapsed from a hamstring injury and had to cross the finish line with the help of his teammates.

In August 2017, following the World Athletics Championships, Bolt announced his retirement from track and field. "For me I don't think one championship is going to change what I've done," he said at a press conference. "I personally won't be one of those persons to come back."

Top ten Usain Bolt quotes

1. "No matter how far you get ahead of me, I'm gonna catch you. That's my mentality that I go there with."
2. "Dreams are free. Goals have a cost. While you can daydream for free, goals don't come without a price. Time, Effort, Sacrifice, and Sweat. How will you pay for your goals?"
3. "Worrying gets you nowhere. If you turn up worrying about how you're going to perform, you've already lost. Train hard, turn up, run your best and the rest will take care of itself."
4. "Don't think about the start of the race, think about the ending."
5. "Easy is not an option. No days off. Never Quit. Be Fearless.. Talent you have Naturally. Skill is only developed by hours and hours of work."
6. "You have to set yourself goals so you can push yourself harder. Desire is the key to success."
7. "Kill them with success and bury them with a smile."
8. "Don't think about the start of the race, think about the ending."
9. "For me, I'm focused on what I want to do. I know what I need to do to be a champion, so I'm working on it."
10. "I try to lead by example."

Determination

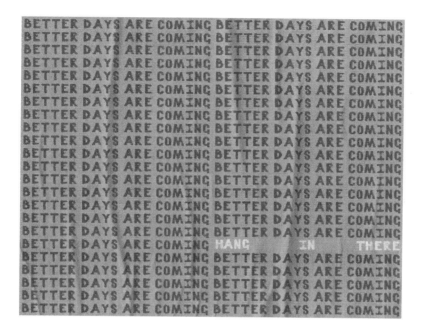

Definition

Determination is defined as a firm intent or a decision which has been reached. An example of employers, **determination** is the strength to keep applying for jobs after being turned down by dozens of potential.

Soichiro Honda

In 1938, Mr Soichiro Honda, was a poor student who had a dream of designing a piston ring that he would sell to and manufacture for Toyoto Corporation. Every day he would go to school, and all night long he would work on his design. He spent what little money he had on his project, and it still wasn't finished. Finally he pawned his wife's jewellery to continue.

After years of effort he finally designed the piston ring he was sure Toyota would buy. When he took it to them, they rejected it. He was sent back to school to suffer the humiliation of his teachers and friends, telling him what an idiot he was for designing such a ridiculous gadget.

Finally, after two more years, he refined his design, and Toyota actually bought it! In order to build his piston factory, Mr Honda needed concrete, but the Japanese government was gearing up for World War Two, so none was available. Once again, it looked as if his dream would die. He got together with his friends, and they worked around the clock trying different approaches until they found a new way to manufacture concrete. He built his factory and was finally able to produce his piston rings.

The story doesn't end here. During the war, the USA bombed his factory, destroying most of it. He rallied his employees and told them to watch where the bombers dropped their fuel cans. He then used the collected cans to help with the raw materials he needed in his manufacturing process, as the raw materials couldn't be obtained in Japan. Finally an earthquake levelled his factory and he was forced to sell his piston operation to Toyota.

When the war ended, Japan was in total turmoil, petrol was so scarce, Mr Honda couldn't even get enough petrol to drive his car to the market to buy food for his family. He then noticed a little motor he had, one which was the size and type to drive a traditional lawnmower, and he got the idea of hooking it up to his bicycle. In that moment, the first motorised bike was created. He drove it to and from the market, and pretty soon is friends were asking him to make some for them, too.

Shortly thereafter, he'd made so many "motorbikes" that he ran out of motors, so he decided to build a new factory to manufacture his own. But he had no money, and Japan was torn apart. How would he do it? He came up with the idea of writing a letter to every bicycle-shop in Japan, telling them about his cheap motorbike. Of the 18,000 bicycle-shop owners who received a letter, 3,000 gave Mr Honda money, and he manufactured his first shipment.

Unfortunately the motorbike was too big and bulky, and very few Japanese bought it. He decided to change his approach again, and stripped the bike down to make it much lighter and smaller. He called it The Cub, and it became an "overnight success," winning Honda the Emperor's Award.

Today, Mr Honda's company is one of the most successful in the world. All because Mr Honda was so **determined** not to give up on his dream and ambition.

Top ten Soichiro Honda quotes

1. "Instead of being afraid of the challenge and failure, be afraid of avoiding the challenge and doing nothing"
2. "Success represents 1% of your work, which results from the 99% of failure"
3. "We only have one future and it will be made of our dreams, if we have the courage to challenge convention"
4. "Many people only dream about success, while for me success is to overcome permanent failures"
5. "Hope makes you forget all the difficult hours"
6. "My biggest thrill is when I plan something and it fails. My mind is then filled with ideas of how I can improve it"
7. "Man is not interesting without some imperfection"
8. "The value of life can be measured by how many times your soul has been deeply stirred"
9. "Enjoying your work is essential. If your work becomes an extension of your own ideas, you will surely enjoy it"
10. "The day I stop dreaming is the day I die"

Motivation

Definition

Motivation is the process that initiates, guides, and maintains goal-oriented behaviors. It is what causes you to act, whether it is getting a glass of water to reduce thirst or reading a book to gain knowledge.

Anthony Robbins

Robbins was born Anthony J. Mahavoric in North Hollywood, California. His surname was originally spelled 'Mohorović' and is of Croatian origin.[4] Robbins is the eldest of three children and his parents divorced when he was 7. His mother then had a series of husbands, including Jim Robbins, a former semi-professional baseball player who legally adopted Anthony when he was 12.

His father could not provide for their family, so he left them. His mother started abusing alcohol and prescription drugs sometime after. While growing up, Robbins helped provide for his siblings. Robbins was raised in Azusa and Glendora, California. He was elected student body president in his senior year and grew 10 inches in high school, a growth spurt later attributed to a pituitary tumour. He has said his home life was "chaotic" and "abusive." When he was 17 years old, Robbins' mother chased him out of the house with a knife, and he never returned. Robbins later worked as a janitor, and did not attend college.

Robbins began his career promoting seminars for Jim Rohn.

Later, without any educational background in psychology, Robbins began his own work as a self-help coach. He taught neurolinguistic programming (NLP) and Ericksonian hypnosis after training with NLP co-founder John Grinder. In 1983, Robbins learned to firewalk and began to incorporate it into his seminars. Robbins' use of board breaking, skydiving, and later firewalking in his seminars is intended to help participants learn to push through their fears.

Robbins promoted his services as a "peak performance coach" through his books and TV infomercials. His first infomercial, *Personal Power*, was released in 1988 and produced by Guthy Renker. Early infomercials featured celebrities such as Pro Football Hall of Fame quarterback Fran Tarkenton and actor Martin Sheen. By 1991, an estimated 100 million Americans in 200 media markets had viewed his infomercials.

Robbins has written three best-selling books: *Unlimited Power*, *Awaken the Giant Within*, and *Money: Master the Game*.

Unlimited Power, published in 1986, discusses the topics of health and energy, overcoming fears, persuasive communication, and enhancing relationships.[14] In the book, Robbins argues that by using neuro-linguistic programming "anyone can become successful at almost anything." According to Magill Book Reviews, Robbins develops "a systematic framework for directing our own brain."

Awaken the Giant Within, published in 1991, according to *The New York Times*, the book contains "ways to take control of your emotional, physical and financial destiny." In 1994, Robbins published *Giant Steps*, a daily instructional book, in a pocket size. His third best-seller, *Money: Master the Game*, was published in 2014, reached number one on the *New York Times*' "Advice, How-To, & Miscellaneous" bestseller list in December 2014, and went on to sell a million copies in its first year.[18] The book contains information stemming from his interviews with over 50 financial experts.

Top ten Anthony Robbins quotes

1. "At any moment, the decision you make can change the course of your life forever"
2. "I challenge you to make your life a masterpiece. I challenge you to join the ranks of those people who live what they teach, who walk their talk"
3. "Goals are like magnets. They'll attract the things that make them come true"
4. "The only impossible journey is the one you never begin"
5. "If you talk about it, it's a dream, if you envision it, it's possible but if you schedule it, it's real"
6. "Focus on where you want to go, not on what you fear"
7. "There is no such thing as failure, only results"
8. "Don't try to be perfect! Just be an excellent example of being human"
9. "Stop being afraid of what could go wrong, and start being excited of what could go right"
10. "We can change our lives. We can do, have, and be exactly what we wish."

Made in the USA
Columbia, SC
28 September 2020